SIMPLE MACHINES

PULLEYS

Nancy Dickmann

BROWN BEAR BOOKS

Published by Brown Bear Books Ltd
4877 N. Circulo Bujia
Tucson, AZ 85718
USA

and

Leroy House
436 Essex Rd
London N1 3QP
UK

ISBN 978-1-78121-399-5 (library bound)
ISBN 978-1-78121-429-9 (paperback)

Library of Congress Cataloging-in-Publication Data available on request

Text: Nancy Dickmann
Design Manager: Keith Davis
Picture Manger: Sophie Mortimer
Editorial Director: Lindsey Lowe
Children's Publisher: Anne O'Daly

Manufactured in the United States of America
CPSIA compliance information: Batch#AG/5608

Picture Credits
The photographs in this book are used by permission and through the courtesy of:

Front Cover: Dreamstime: main; Shutterstock: Chris Warham bl.
Interior: Alamy: Art Directors & Trip 8–9, Ingolf Pompe 4; Dreamstime: Scott Dali 20t, Christian Delbert 12–13, Helgidinson 15, Ricardo Toledo 4–5; istockphoto: 6–7, 10–11, mage Source 14, listinbids 18, People Images 16–17, Jordi Ramisa 21t, Doug Schneider Photo 16, The Palmer 1, 6, Wavebreak media 20r, YinYang 17; Shutterstock: guellermo Celano 12, Jacek Chabraszewski 20–21, nikkytok 21b; Thinkstock: istockphoto 14–15, 18–19.

t-top, r-right, l-left, c-center, b-bottom

Brown Bear Books has made every attempt to contact the copyright holder. If you have any information please contact: licensing@brownbearbooks.co.uk

Websites
The website addresses in this book were valid at the time of going to press. However, it is possible that contents or addresses may change following publication of this book. No responsibility for any such changes can be accepted by the author or the publisher. Readers should be supervised when they access the Internet.

Words in **bold** appear in the Useful Words on page 23.

Contents

What Is a Pulley? 4
What Are Machines? 6
Pulleys and Forces 8
Working Together 10
Pulleys in the Past 12
Types of Pulleys 14
Everyday Pulleys 16
Compound Machines 18
Spot the Pulley! 20
Try It! 22
Useful Words 23
Find out More 24
Index 24

What Is a Pulley?

A pulley looks simple.
It is a wheel with a rope looped over it.
But a pulley can do something amazing.
It can help you lift heavy objects.

A flagpole has a pulley at the top. You pull on the rope. This raises the flag.

An **axle** is a rod. It goes through the pulley's wheel. The wheel spins around the axle. The wheel's edges usually stick out a little bit. They keep the rope from slipping off.

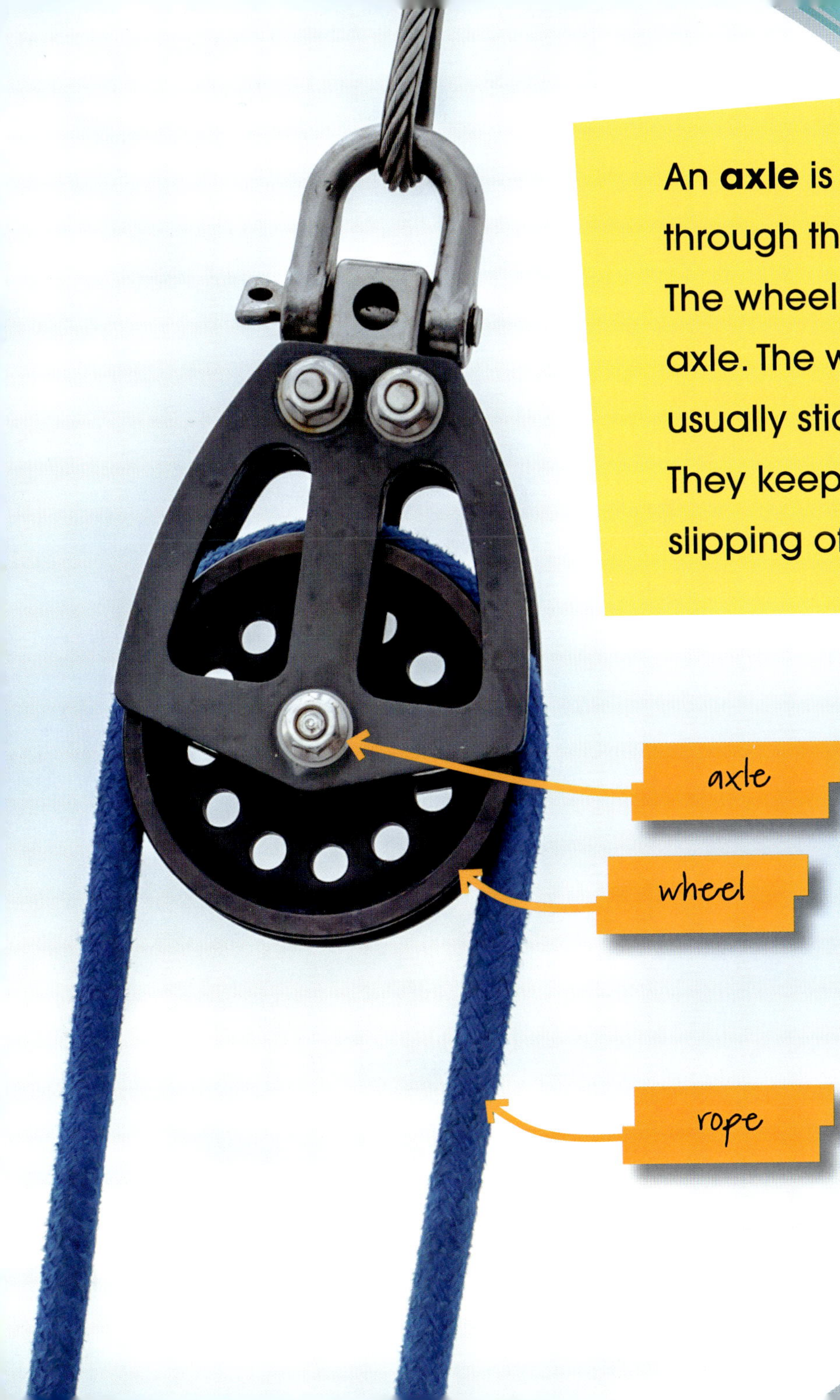

What Are Machines?

A pulley is a type of **machine**.
Machines help us do work.
We need energy to move or lift things.
Machines make the job easier.
They can make a **force** more powerful.

A zip line uses a pulley. The pulley runs along a cable.

Some machines are simple.
They only have one part.
A jet engine has many parts.
They work together.

Pulleys and Forces

A **force** is a push or a pull. You pull down on a pulley's rope. The pulley changes the force's direction. The other end of the rope goes up. It lifts a weight.

Pulleys

You can use a pulley to lift something by pulling down.

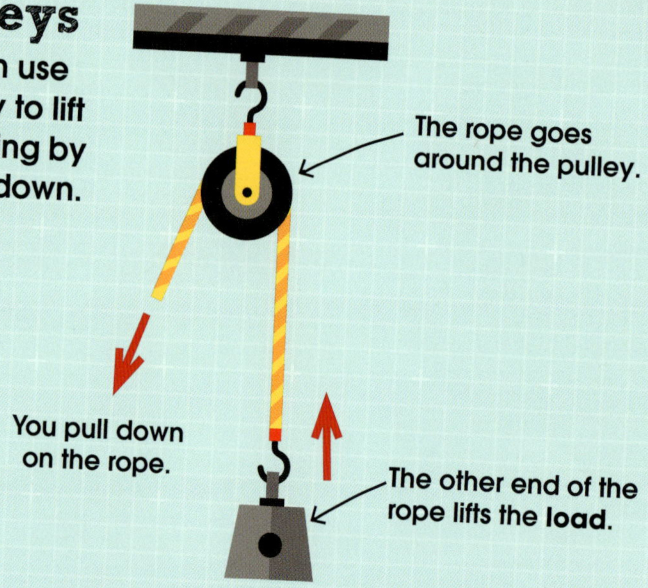

This man is using a single pulley. He pulls on the rope. His muscles supply force. He has to pull hard to lift the bricks.

Working Together

Pulleys can work together. Using more pulleys makes lifting easier. The pulleys make your **force** stronger. You have to pull the rope farther. But you do not need to pull as hard.

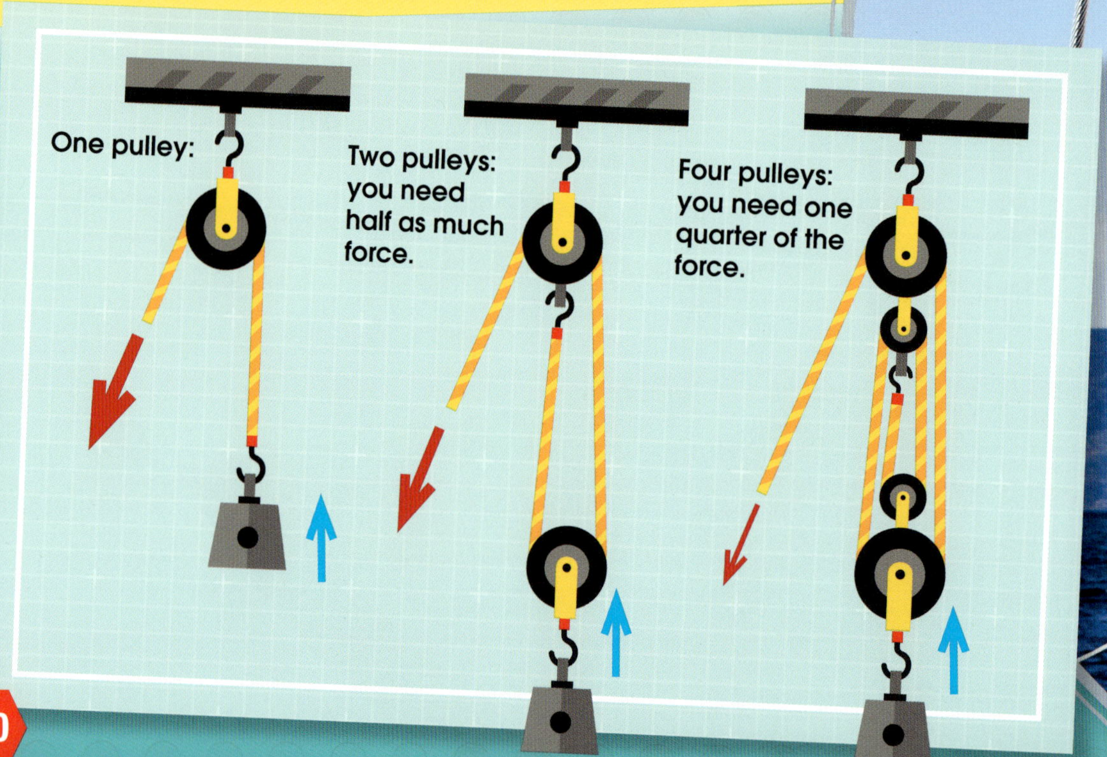

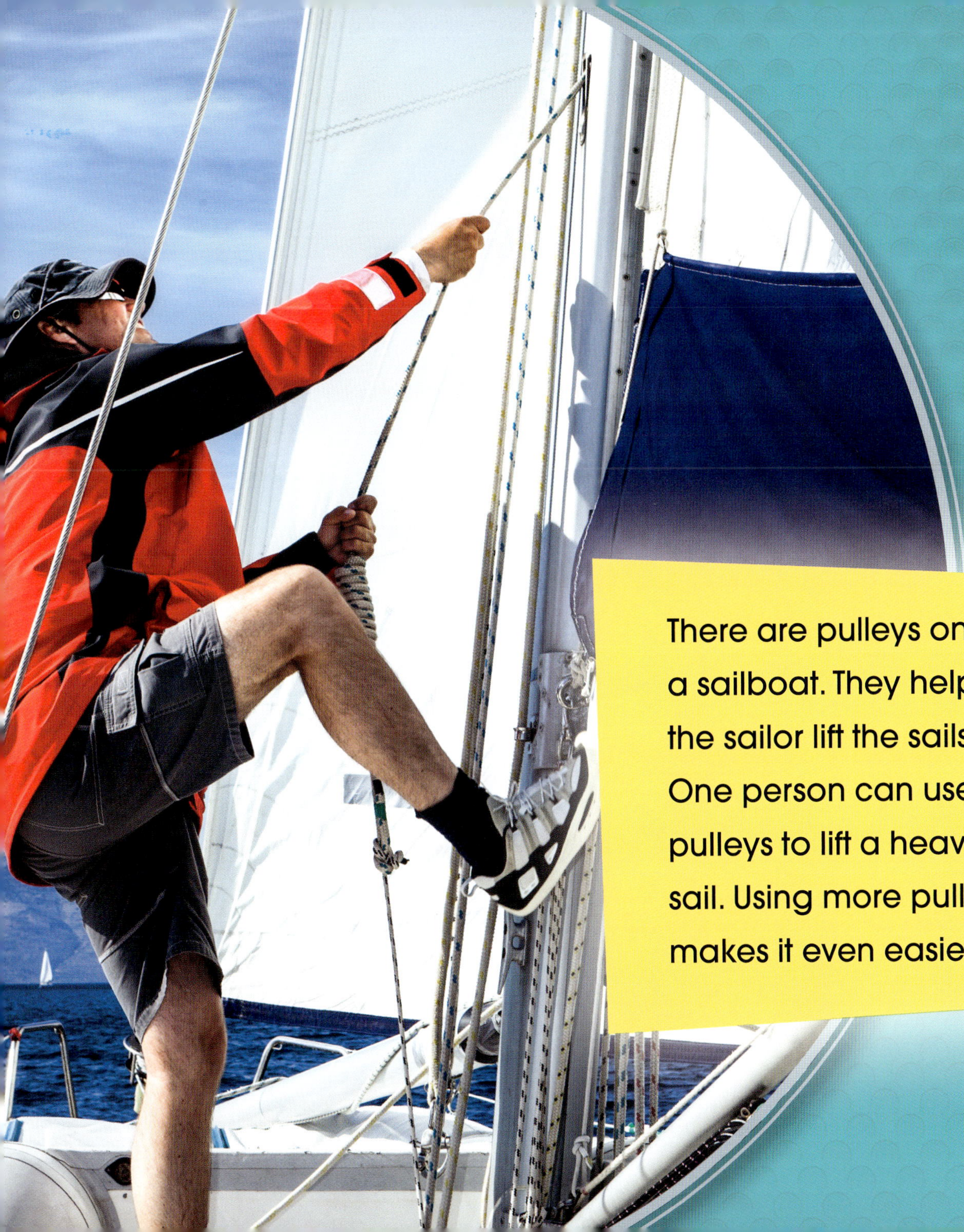

There are pulleys on a sailboat. They help the sailor lift the sails. One person can use pulleys to lift a heavy sail. Using more pulleys makes it even easier.

Pulleys in the Past

No one knows who invented pulleys. Wheels were invented first. Pulleys were used more than 3,000 years ago. They helped lift buckets of water.

Some wells use pulleys. They help raise and lower the bucket.

WOW!

Archimedes was a Greek scientist. Once he used pulleys to move a ship, all by himself!

Armies used these giant catapults to attack castles. Soldiers used a pulley to lift a huge weight. Then they let the weight drop. The catapult threw a heavy stone at the castle walls.

Types of Pulleys

We still use pulleys today. Some elevators have pulleys. A tow truck uses a pulley. There are even pulleys in a car's engine.

Rock climbers use pulleys. The pulleys help them go up or down safely.

Sailboats have pulleys. They are inside a case. The case is called a block.

Cranes lift heavy loads. They use pulleys to help them lift. These pulleys do not use ropes. They have steel cables instead.

Everyday Pulleys

There may be pulleys in your home. Sliding doors run on pulleys. So do some curtains. Some clotheslines have a pulley at each end. That makes it easier to hang out laundry.

Pulleys help you pull the clothesline along. You stand in one place to hang up the clothes.

People lift weights. It makes their muscles stronger. Many gym machines have pulleys. People pull on the cables. The pulleys raise and lower weights smoothly.

Compound Machines

Pulleys are simple machines. So are **levers** and wheels. They can work together. They form compound machines. A lawn mower is a **compound machine**. It has wheels and a pulley. Its blades are **wedges**.

A lawn mower's cord goes around a pulley. You pull the cord to start the engine.

A bicycle is a **machine**. It has pulleys. It has levers, too. The chain is like a pulley. The pedals are levers. Pushing the pedals moves the chain. This makes the wheels spin.

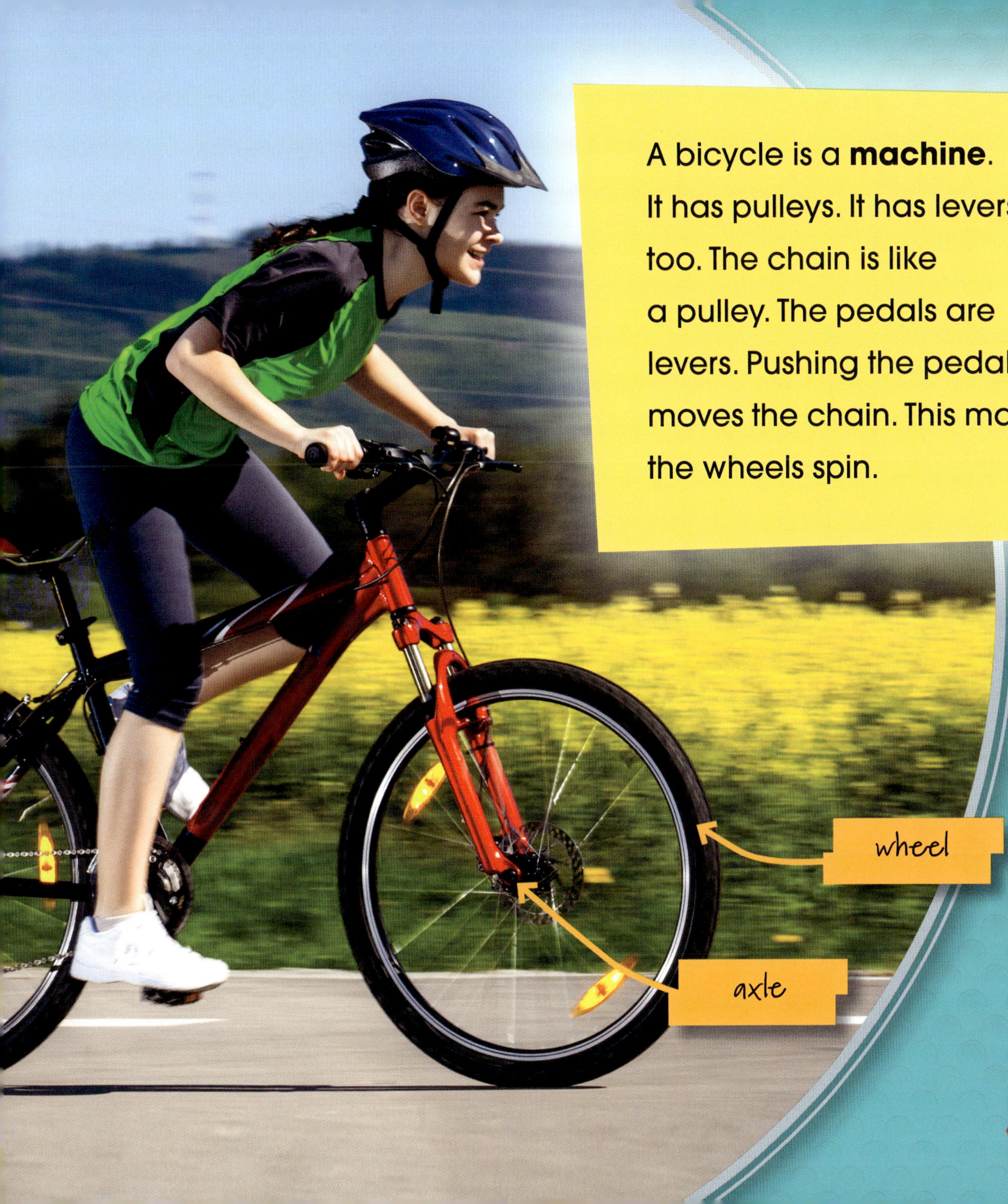

Spot the Pulley!

Can you find the pulleys in these pictures?

1

2

3

5

4

Try It!

Make a pulley, then use it to lift a weight!

You will need:

- **empty spool of thread**
- **pencil or stick that fits through the spool**
- **string**
- **bottle of water**
- **friend to help you**

1. Stick the pencil or stick through the center of the spool.

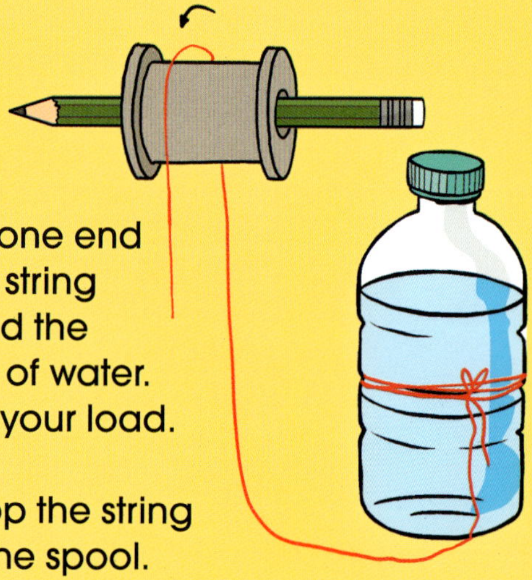

2. Tie one end of the string around the bottle of water. This is your load.

3. Loop the string over the spool.

4. While your friend holds the pencil, pull down on the string.

5. The pulley will spin as you lift the water bottle.

Try adding a second pulley to your setup. Does it make the bottle easier to lift?

Useful Words

axle A rod at the center of a wheel or pulley. The wheel spins around the axle.

compound machine A machine that is made up of smaller machines. It can have several different simple machines.

force A push or a pull.

lever Type of simple machine. A lever has a long beam that rests on a point called a pivot.

load The object that a machine tries to move.

machine Something that helps us do work. Machines use energy to do a job.

wedge A simple machine with angled sides. Wedges can split things apart.

Answers to page 20–21: Did you spot the pulleys? **1.** The hook on the crane; **2.** inside the rowing machine; **3.** the chain on the bicycle; **4.** the starting cord; **5.** the rope goes around a pulley.

Find out More

Websites
www.britannica.com/technology/simple-machine

www.explainthatstuff.com/pulleys.html

www.msichicago.org/play/simplemachines/

Books
Making Machines with Pulleys Chris Oxlade, Raintree 2015

Pulleys Sian Smith, Heinemann-Raintree 2012

Pulleys in Action Gillian Gosman, PowerKids Press 2010

Index

axles 5, 19

blocks 15

cables 6, 15, 17
catapults 13
clotheslines 16
compound machines 18–19
cranes 15

energy 6

forces 6, 8–9, 10

levers 18, 19

machines 6–7, 17, 18, 19
muscles 9, 17

pulling 4, 8, 9, 10, 16, 17, 18

ropes 4, 5, 8, 9, 10, 15

sailboats 11, 15

wedges 18
wheels 4, 5, 12, 18, 19
working together 7, 10–11, 18